Topiary
for Everyone

For MO and JP
who both made this book possible

Topiary
for Everyone

Bobby Meyer

Search Press

First published in Great Britain 1999

Search Press Limited
Wellwood, North Farm Road,
Tunbridge Wells, Kent TN2 3DR

Text copyright © Bobby Meyer 1999

Photographs by Bobby Meyer
Design copyright © Search Press Ltd. 1999

ISBN 0 85532 882 7

The author has made every effort to contact copyright holders of photographs reproduced in this book. Any omissions will be rectified in subsequent printings if notice is given to the author.

Colour separation by P&W Graphics, Singapore
Printed in Spain by Elkar S. Coop. Bilbao 48012

Page 1 *Elizabeth Braimbridge, specialist box grower, clipping a box spiral.*

Page 2 *I never fail to be amused when I drive past this quirky yew topiary in a front garden near my home. Rather than cut it back harder when growth expanded beyond the garden wall, the owner simply allowed it to do what comes naturally (to a yew tree, that is) and let the lamp post fall into its green embrace.*

Page 3 *Chess set at Brickwall House, Northiam, East Sussex. The yew is grown through the custom-made metal frames representing life-size chess figures, set each in their own square of coloured gravel. It is then clipped back so that it is just proud of these frames.*

Contents

Introduction   6

History   8

Box   12

Yew   20

Other Topiary Plants   36

Instant Topiary Gardens   48

Creating a Garden with Topiary   52

A Pair of Acorns   56

Clipping Bay Laurel Topiary   62

Bizarre Topiary   66

Wondrous Creatures   76

Making a Spiral   84

Acknowledgments   90

Gardens to Visit   92

Index   94

Bibliography   96

Introduction

My fascination with topiary has grown out of two separate strands in my life: gardening and photography. As often happens, my own first serious foray into caring for topiary, and from there moving into creating my own designs, was almost accidental. Twenty years ago I moved to a house in the country and was immediately faced with the task of taming a badly neglected garden, stifled by huge overgrown hedges of hawthorn and yew. It was only after an initial cutting programme that I was able to see the potential for building on the existing planting, and designing my own topiary garden.

I visited other gardens with topiary for inspiration and encouragement, enjoying the sense of discovery, and so began to shape my own ideas. Travelling around, I also used my camera to capture the variety and wealth of inspiring topiary creations, whether in the grounds of grand houses or in the tiny front gardens of London terraces. Through the detail of photography I came to realise that, no matter how modest in design or size, each clipped shape is the very personal expression of the individual who wields the shears or hedgecutters. That is perhaps the essence of topiary's very particular appeal. How exciting that this creative outlet is open to anyone and that there are no rules – it is up to you to give the plant movement and shape.

Without realising it at the time, I was well and truly hooked on the subject and as I travelled around Europe my slide archive of topiary shapes and designs was growing.

In this book I would like to share this pleasure in designing, growing and creating topiary shapes. It is not always easy to show how it is done, but I have tried to include a selection of 'action shots' which I hope will inspire the more timid amongst you. I have also concentrated on selecting photographs of lesser known gardens, both public and private, and hope you will enjoy the element of quirky humour which topiary can display so well.

This medley of strange rounded shapes, all of different heights, is in the extensive grounds of Elvaston Castle in Derbyshire. They seem to pile into one another in a disconcerting yet rhythmic manner. The unusual contrast between the dark green and the less commonly-used golden yew makes the plant forms seem even more alive. The result is similar to a beautiful sculpture, something almost from another world. Although there was a detailed planting plan for Elvaston's original topiary in the nineteenth century, in compositions such as these I suspect that it was up to different gardeners over the years to produce such individual shapes and the unusual effect we can enjoy today.

History

Topiary has been in and out of fashion for well over two thousand years, if not longer. We know that the Romans were very competitive about clipping plants such as box, myrtle and cypress into fanciful shapes. The diarist, Pliny the Younger (61–113AD) has left us enthusiastic and detailed accounts of hunting scenes, ships and animals all clipped out of cypress. In letters to friends, he vividly describes his own beautiful gardens outside Rome, boasting of animals and shapes of all kinds clipped out of what was probably box – even his own initials and his gardeners' were 'growing' in his terraced grounds.

We now also have concrete evidence that the Romans brought the art of topiary with them when they settled and built their villas and palaces in Britain. Close to the city of Chichester in West Sussex, you can visit the site of Fishbourne Palace, the remains of the largest Roman building yet to be found North of the Alps, where evidence of extensive formal gardens has been uncovered. Digging deep down until they reached clay, archaeologists found the beautifully preserved layout

An unusual way of cutting initials out of a topiary shape at Clipsham, close to Stretton in Rutland. This cone is one of an avenue of nearly one hundred and fifty yews (thought to be over two hundred years old) which formed a unique carriage drive leading up to Clipsham Hall. The trimming of the yew trees was begun in 1870 when the Clipsham Estate Head Forester, Amos Alexander, living in the gatehouse, began creating figures out of the yew trees as a hobby.

Opposite *The original seventeenth-century Baroque gardens at William and Mary's Royal Palace, Het Loo, East Holland, disappeared in the early 1800s, overlaid by an English landscape garden which was then fashionable. Between 1977 and 1984 the gardens were restored to the original design of Daniel Marot and have now matured, to be enjoyed once again in all their former splendour.*

It is quite a special experience to walk around the replanted formal box gardens of the Roman Palace excavated at Fishbourne (near Chichester, West Sussex). Designed by an anonymous Roman, perhaps even the owner of the palace, it is possibly the only garden of its type in Britain, where the original Roman planting plan was followed once excavations were completed in the 1960s.

of the original box gardens still intact. New box was grown following the original ancient planting scheme and today we are able to enjoy this Roman garden as it once was. The elaborate design is on a large scale, often comprising three parallel rows placed close together and already foretelling the patterns which the Renaissance Italians were to use in their grand palace gardens many centuries later.

There are no records of topiary after the Romans left Britain or during the Dark Ages. In fact, there is nothing until Medieval times, when illuminated manuscripts from around the thirteenth century began recording monastic and outdoor life. Gardens were shown with neatly-trimmed plants, possibly box, myrtle or rosemary, used as low hedging around beds of flowers or herbs.

A century or so later, during the Italian Renaissance, gardens had become more sophisticated. Designs were often based on popular knot patterns inspired by contemporary textiles, wood carvings and plaster decoration. They reflected the new thinking where gardens were no longer just a practical necessity for growing food but were part of an overall decorative scheme.

Low hedges of clipped box and myrtle were most commonly used for creating complex geometrical designs – either enclosing beds of flowers, or as part of a grander overall scheme made up of intricate patterns. Many were so grand and complex that they were conceived to be viewed from an upper floor of the villa or palace. Some of these designs still exist today, for example, at the Villa Lanta, Bagnaia. As there was only a limited range of plants available at that time, box and myrtle were clipped into ornate and architectural shapes, such as pyramids, globes, obelisks, animals and ships.

Today, elaborate and inventive topiary is at its most prolific in the Netherlands, and Dutch growers can trace their topiary history back to the fifteenth century. Since that time they have been producing wonderful clipped topiary on a large scale and today the tradition continues, with Boskoop being a major centre for box nurseries. The restored gardens of the royal palace Het Loo, in East Holland, are a splendid example of the beauty and complexity of the gardens which existed in the Netherlands in the seventeenth century.

Fashions in garden design spread swiftly around Europe with travelling craftsmen, artists and designers/builders being much in demand at the English Court. Seventeenth- and eighteenth-century engravings show that gardens in England followed the current fashions closely and that they had topiary to match that of anywhere else in Europe. Some of the designs were quite fantastic, as engravings from this period show (see pages 92–95), with huge tunnels, hedge screens pierced with arches at short intervals and other large-scale projects. In the Netherlands and England, nurseries supplied trees and plants in huge numbers. The craze for topiary finally peaked during the reign of William and Mary (1688–1702).

Meanwhile, in seventeenth-century France, magnificent formal gardens were created by Le Nôtre and his followers. Extensive use was made of clipped yews and box for parterres, broderies, obelisks and pyramids. These all relied on an army of gardeners to keep their strict shapes, and formed not only a wonderful foil for the château or palace itself, but also a stark formal contrast with the woods and grassy avenues beyond the formal gardens.

An unusual design for box, in the extensive, historical gardens of Chiswick House, West London. The pattern is full of movement and somehow calls to mind the slices of a swiss roll!

Box

There are far more varieties of box than are generally realised (possibly over eighty), but *Buxus sempervirens* is the most commonly found and easiest to grow in Europe. Although it likes the hot sun (when its characteristic pungent smell is strongest) it can be grown both in dry areas such as Italy, and in the wetter and colder climates of England and the Netherlands.

Box lends itself particularly well to low topiary, especially hedging in knot gardens and parterres. It can be trained into spirals, and is very effective in simple shapes such as cones and balls. It has also been used for sundials, with the numerals and gnomon being in box and the dial filled with light–coloured gravel to enable the shadow to show clearly.

Knot Gardens

Knot gardens probably evolved from medieval kitchen gardens where medicinal and culinary herbs had to be kept separate from each other. They were very popular in the sixteenth and seventeenth centuries, and took several forms. The low box edging, in the form of knots or interlocking geometric shapes, surrounded flowering plants, gravel or other stones, or grass.

The early American colonists brought the idea of knot gardens with them, perhaps finding that they were a symbol of order in the surrounding untamed land. Thomas Jefferson's father owned a plantation at Tuckahoe in which there was no less than a whole acre of knot garden. The box hedges, laid out in ovals and concentric circles, would have extended one-and-a-half miles if placed in a straight line.

Parterres

Similar to knot gardens but larger in scale, these were much developed by the French, who frequently added to existing formal gardens during this period. By the early 1700s, three distinct types had appeared:

parterres de broderie consisting of box edging and coloured earth in an imitation of embroidery

parterres à l'anglaise where the box was used to edge turf cut into patterns

parterres of cut work where the box outlines were filled with flowers

Opposite The stunning effect of these Baroque parterre shapes in the gardens of Het Loo, East Holland, speaks for itself. A modern garden design could successfully reinterpret this concept.

Opposite inset A newly planted knot garden using very small box plants. Within a year or two this will have filled in sufficiently to already give shape to the design.

Box is not just green! This field of young box plants clearly demonstrates the wide range of colour tones there are, which can be used to good effect when designing a new box garden.

Enthusiasm for parterres was widespread during the 1700s. Records show that they existed in Germany, Sweden, Spain and Portugal as well as France and England. The idea even spread to China.

Some parterres may still be seen today. There are famous box parterres at Seaton Delaval Hall in Northumberland and at Pitmedden, in Aberdeenshire, for example, the Scottish National Trust has a partly-original, partly-modern, box-edged parterre, in an attempt to emulate what the seventeenth-century originator might have done with modern plants. However, many more parterres of this period have been lost. The heyday of formal gardens and topiary, during the reign of William and Mary, came to an end with the return to 'natural' landscaping. Blenheim originally had much parterre work, designed by Henry Wise, but this was removed by 'Capability' Brown (the existing parterres are Edwardian).

This bizarre box figure appears to have been achieved by patient and careful use of wire, which pulls stems together into the desired shape, and possibly also some chicken wire to create the bulky parts, through which the plants then can grow.

Box in pots

Box is frequently grown in pots, the advantage being you are able to move the pots according to the season or simply to vary your garden scheme. Success with such moveable topiary depends on regular attention.

Particular care must be taken while watering. You cannot rely on rain to do this for you, because it fails to penetrate the foliage to any extent, so make sure that the plant has water even during wet spells. It helps to place pots on terracotta saucers.

Plants should also be fed regularly from early spring to mid-August; be careful how you do this, as the leaves can be burnt easily by fertilizer.

Box usually needs re-potting every three years. When choosing the new pot, remember to allow for plenty of room around the rootball.

Clipping

Freshly cut box is very susceptible to frostburn, so do not be tempted to cut too early in the year. Ideally, you should clip twice a year but it is better to restrict yourself to one annual clipping if you live in an area where late frosts are likely. In most areas, early to mid-June is a suitable time for the first cut.

It is very tempting to start trimming earlier, as box can quickly look shaggy once the new bright green leaves appear on the darker winter foliage. But wait, and remind yourself that a late frost could leave you with a badly scorched plant which could take a long time to recover.

There is also the danger of early autumn frosts, and so the second cut should take place before the end of August. This clipping should be just a good tidy-up to enable the plants to retain their shape throughout the winter.

The best tool for cutting box is a pair of ordinary garden shears or sheep shears, although an electric hedge-cutter may be used – with care – on established topiary. A handy, old-fashioned, tip is to use a string tied between two poles as a guide. Stretch it just below the desired trimming line and be careful not to cut into it. Aim to cut on a line within the old growth as the soft new leaves are easily damaged. Never clip on a hot day as the newly-cut areas are liable to scorching.

It is also possible to to 'pluck' the plant by pulling out individual twigs by hand. This gives a rather fluffy effect which can be an interesting contrast to the more formal method of clipping topiary.

In this box garden the unusual curved pattern creates a rhythm and movement which contrasts splendidly with the neat, geometric shapes opposite.

A box 'curl' virtually comes alive! It looks equally stunning whether placed in the middle of a lawn or on a gravelled area and is an excellent opportunity to make the most of golden or variegated varieties of box.

Opposite *A field of semi-surreal shapes in box. This extraordinary sight leaves all visitors feeling inspired to attempt their own fantasies in box.*

Part of a box parterre in the garden of the Frans Hals Museum, Haarlem, Holland.

Yew

Yew makes an excellent, dark green, dense hedge and can be used very successfully for cutting into a wide range of bold topiary shapes which lend great charm and mystery to a garden. Simple, classic yew hedging can transform a garden at a relatively low cost compared with, say, building brick walls in the same area. It acts as an extremely effective wind-barrier and it is an undemanding plant when it comes to maintenance.

And yet, for all its versatility, yew does not always have the reputation it deserves. For some, it is a reminder of churchyards, gloom and mortality. For others, their immediate response is to point out how slowly it grows – but this is not true at all.

Yews do indeed frequently grow in churchyards – often wonderful, ancient specimens, with characteristic reddish, soft bark. It is said that some of these yews were planted by our pagan ancestors, before the churches themselves were even built. Recently, scientists have been talking about some yews perhaps being up to 4,000 years old. Yew is an amazing tree, part of our heritage, and to my mind not at all depressing.

If you buy English yew bare-rooted, that is not in a container, then plant as soon as possible. Make sure the roots are protected from any frost in the meantime, by either wrapping in sacking or heeling-in until they can be planted out in their final position. Height is not always important – look for bushy growth all the way up the stem which will provide the foundation for a healthy, thick hedge.

Opposite *Newly-clipped, bold, crisp shapes forming a gateway at Goddards in Surrey (house and garden designed by Sir Edwin Lutyens and Gertrude Jekyll). The head gardener assured me that the rich deep green of all his hedges was thanks to an annual dose of fertilizer.*

The dense green of a simple yew hedge can be accentuated by simply placing a statue or painted garden seat (or both, as in this Sussex garden) either in front of, or in a niche cut out of the hedge.

Growth rates for yew plants are good – between 23–46cm (9–18in) per year. In *Yew and Box*, Nathaniel Lloyd describes a twelve-year trial involving the planting of eight different yew hedges with plants of different shapes and heights, in a range of soil types. Interestingly, the conclusion was that bigger does not necessarily mean better. The smaller, uniformly well-grown plants produced a better, thicker hedge more quickly than the larger plants – the latter had a more uneven growth and they were only bushy at the top.

When selecting plants for a hedge it is important to choose yews which are bushy right down the plant stem. In this trial, the bushy 1m (3ft) high pyramid-shaped yews grew into a solid hedge within less than four years. A point worth noting is that the cheaper, smaller plants, around 0.3m (1ft) high caught up with the 1m (3ft) high plants within nine years!

Opposite A winning contrast between the soft-edged purple peephole – created expressly to provide a tempting view to the garden room beyond – and the deliberate, solidly geometric shape of the yew seen in the middle distance, itself forming a contrast with a delightful loose texture of flowers in the middleground.

Of all the plant sizes, the smallest ones suffered least loss and were the easiest to establish. So patience is indeed rewarded.

More recently, Dr Roy Strong, writing in *Creating Small Gardens*, described making a new hedge with plants only 46cm (18in) high. Twelve years later, he was sitting in his garden enclosed by the resulting magnificent 2.5m (8ft) high hedge, which he had shaped into stunning architectural piers and buttresses.

English yew

There are many different yew varieties, but it is the Common or English Yew (*Taxus baccata*) which is most widely used for hedging and topiary. English Yew is an evergreen conifer, which can grow to more than 6m (20ft), is very hardy and fairly undemanding, liking sun or shade. Its leaves are glossy and dark green and it has deep red, rather translucent, curiously-shaped berries which are poisonous. Yew tolerates most soils, including heavy clay, although it does prefer not to have its roots standing in water. It is rarely affected by disease – over a period of twenty years my vast, ninety-year-old yew hedge never once had any problems, except in extreme years of drought when its obvious suffering was relieved by watering regularly.

Golden yew

The Golden yew, *Taxus aurea,* is just as handsome as English yew. It can be used for hedging and topiary, although hedging is not seen that often. It can look particularly good clipped into rounded shapes such as huge globes, sitting on the ground, or against a dark green background of English yew (see page 33).

Yew as topiary

Because it responds so well to hard and regular pruning, yew is ideal topiary material. The main cut is best done once a year, around the end of August and certainly well before the first autumn frosts, to allow the plant a little time to recover before the cold weather sets in. This ensures that it will keep a good firm shape well into the following summer.

The dense, dark green winter foliage changes as new growth sprouts in April/May, showing a pleasing, bright green outer layer which can almost give a halo-effect. Depending on how much new growth appears, some gardeners like to give yew a light clip in June to avoid a rather shaggy look towards the end of the season, and also to lighten the work when doing the main annual cut.

The most common use for yew is as a boundary hedge, either along the garden perimeter or as a divider, to section off different areas of the garden to create distinct 'rooms'. Yew makes a stunning backdrop for colourful flowerbeds and at the same time doubles as good protection against damaging winds.

For the more architecturally-minded, the yew hedge is a great starting point for creative additions. These could be buttresses, which might be used to divide up a long herbaceous border, castellations or other decorative features on top of the hedge, or archways cut into the hedge which lead through to other parts of the garden. Niches cut into the hedge come into their own when used for stone statuary or place a white-painted garden seat in front, for a stunning contrast. More whimsically, a circular cut-out window can provide a view out into the countryside beyond. Yew hedges can be used for a maze or the wings of a garden theatre. The possibilities are endless!

When creating a new design, take time to think also about the effect of light and shadow which is particularly striking with such a densely green plant as yew. Deep crenellations are very effective, creating a chequered pattern in certain lights, and the long shadows cast by yew topiary shapes over a lawn on a late autumn afternoon are just wonderful.

Yew also lends itself well to repetition of shape. So, for instance, an avenue of yew cones planted at fairly close intervals can be most striking. A row of huge golden globes can look almost alive, producing an eerie feeling of movement.

In general, yew hedges have a strong, square cross-section, but there are other alternatives to choose from. A slight 'batter', i.e. where the base is wider than the top, looks very smart and gives the bottom section of the plant a chance to get more light. The result is improved growth at the base, which can otherwise get a bit thin. In fact, I have noticed that in Belgium a generally narrower, 'battered' hedge shape is quite common.

You may be lucky enough to have inherited an existing old yew hedge when you moved house. But, more often than not, the hedge will have been neglected and it will need careful restoration.

First aid treatment can simply mean cutting out a bit of dead wood and giving the

Two very unusual clipped yew shapes, in a Dutch country garden, above, and an English garden, below. They look particularly dramatic when the shapes are highlighted in winter frost or snow.

Both this photograph and the one above show how effective the play of light and shadow can be on sharply-clipped yew. The unusual key-hole shape is quite a challenge!

This splendid architectural use of yew hedging is very appealing. The buttresses dividing up the herbaceous border are very easy to create and the golden yew cube sets off the total concept to perfection.

hedge or topiary an extra careful clip in August. However, as I experienced, you could also find yourself faced with reviving a hedge that has suffered such a long period of neglect that drastic action is needed.

My 45m (150ft) long hedge was almost 6m (20ft) tall, had lost all its original shape and reminded me more of a weird caterpillar snaking its way down the garden. It was also asphyxiating the garden and such plants as had survived.

My first step was to cut the hedge back drastically in height, thus allowing light into the centre which had very sparse growth. In fact, in some parts there was so much dead wood that I decided to cut back one side to the stem of the plant. It takes steely nerves to do this, but in most cases the long-term result is worth it. If the condition of the hedge is very bad indeed, you may have to cut back one side hard, wait until there is some regrowth and then cut back the other side. This method will help to keep the shock to the plant to a minimum.

***Opposite** This fastigiate Irish Yew is probably suffering from neglect rather than disease. For the brave-hearted, severe cutting back is usually the best option, as shown in the inset photograph.*

Nowadays there are a number of theories as to how best to tackle neglected or partly-dead yew plants. Pruning expert, David Joyce, in his new book *Topiary and the Art of Training Plants,* suggests that drastic pruning to renovate yew should be carefully planned in stages over several years. He advocates tackling first one side and then the other, after an interval of a year or more to give the plant a chance to recover. Interestingly, he also suggests the plant should be mulched and fertilised a year before starting the cutting back programme.

Once the hedge has thrown out new shoots and achieved the height and cross-section you are aiming for, then it is worth thinking about whether you want to add something interesting or amusing on top.

I decided on a row of bobbles at regular intervals and to achieve this, selected strong upright stems or 'leaders' which were left to sprout when the main cut was done. Eventually the growth on the leaders filled in and it

Piet Oudolf's stunningly original yew topiary design has the mysterious feeling of a maze, yet must in part have been inspired by open-air theatres. The clever positioning (fitting into a narrow space at the end of the garden) combines perfectly with the surprise design element to give the composition an extra dimension.

Overleaf *In the main illustration the choice of more sophisticated equipment, such as this platform lift, enables the owner single-handed to tackle what used to take an army of gardeners. During the Second World War the massive yew hedges, shown inset, were left untrimmed because of labour shortage. When later it came to the 'big cut' it was decided to follow the line of humps and bumps resulting from the years of neglect. They have now become a major visitor attraction.*

An impressive column of giant yew cones. Today they are so huge that the space remaining in between each of them is disproportionately small.

was then quite easy to trim them into the shape I had in mind.

If you are more daring and skilled, you could consider images on top of the hedge, such as foxes being chased by hounds, or peacocks with their distinctive shape. One of my favourite gardens has a huge avenue of yew hedges with extraordinary crowns on top, commemorating a royal anniversary.

Just as effective, however, are architect-ural features or simple stepped levels, which immediately give the hedge an extra dimension and rely on a good eye and precision meas-uring rather than more artistic skills!

Yew responds well to feeding, either with farmyard manure, bonemeal or proprietary brands. They are best transplanted between mid-October to mid-November, giving time to settle over the winter months and they benefit from mulching in dry weather.

Golden yew topiary provides a welcome bright spot in the winter. Here at Elvaston Castle, Derbyshire, a large quantity of golden yew has been used in the design of the topiary gardens.

This photograph shows the unusual contrast between the severe formality of an immaculately clipped yew obelisk and the loose charm of red nasturtium grown as a climber up painted poles.

Opposite *A perfect geometric composition in yew topiary shapes.*

Other Topiary Plants

Many different plants are used in topiary. Here are just a few of the most common ones after yew and box, but it is well worth experimenting with less usual plants such as honeysuckle or the evergreen holm oak.

Hawthorn

This fast-growing, disease-resistant tree is very attractive when grown in mophead shapes in avenues. The pink-flowering variety, *Crataegus laevigata*, is particularly favoured.

These hawthorns have been clipped into mopheads. Although deciduous, the globe shapes are still very striking when leafless over the winter months.

Opposite *Two birds cut out of wild hawthorn bushes beside a Dutch canal. Their creator designed them to face the garden, with their backs to the water, but passers-by also perceive them as leaning towards the canal.*

A mixture of green and golden privet, wittily clipped into a shape reminiscent of a Henry Moore reclining sculpture!

When this house changed hands the new owner set to and came up with an original idea for livening up an otherwise fairly run-of-the-mill privet hedge. He allowed strong leaders to continue growing when clipping and gradually cut the resulting bushy growth into these charming mushroom shapes.

VICTORIA ROAD

This castellated privet hedge is nearly 3.5m (12ft) high. To maintain the crispness of the dramatic outline, it should be clipped at least three times a year.

Privet

This fast-growing, undemanding shrub is very flexible and suitable for any size of garden. It is useful for the novice topiary enthusiast, as any 'mistakes' made will soon grow out...

Privet does need a lot of cutting. Depending on the weather and rainfall, it will need trimming two to three times a year for a good neat finish. There are two varieties, the common dark green and the golden privet. If left untrimmed for any length of time it will produce a fragrant white blossom in spring.

Professionals trimming the hedge shown above using an electric hedge-cutter. They are standing on a small platform for safety.

Portuguese laurel

This very underrated plant grows relatively quickly and takes to being clipped into simple round or square shapes. As seen in the photo right, it looks very good as a standard, but can also be used for cylindrical or dome shapes. Recently I saw a pair growing in square terracotta pots, shaped as tall cones and covered in sprays of berries, which made them look delightful.

Bay laurel

Although the branches are fairly thick and the leaves quite substantial, bay laurel is surprisingly easy to clip into shapes (see pages 62–65) and is often grown as a mophead or globe.

It can also be grown to good effect in containers – a very useful feature in frost-prone areas. Since bay is hardy to only -5°C (23°F) and is liable to scorch in cold winds, as a general rule it must be moved under cover in severe winters.

If you are lucky enough to have a healthy bay tree growing in your garden, try clipping it into a less commonly used cylindrical shape.

Pyracantha/Firethorn

A member of the rose family, the prickly firethorn needs special care when trimming. However, the glossy evergreen leaves, complemented by a froth of small white flowers in spring (pictured top right), followed by a mass of red berries in autumn (pictured bottom right) make up for its thorniness. It grows well against a house wall or shed as shown here, where it has formed a pleasing deep frame surrounding the tiny window – with a particularly amusing reflection when it catches the light.

40

An imposing pair of tightly-clipped golden spirals created from an unusual choice of topiary plant ('Chamaecyparis 'Golden King')in the gardens of Cabbages and Kings, Hadlow Down, East Sussex. They come from Italy and are around twenty five years old.

This hornbeam stilt hedge, at Ham House in Surrey, is grown as a tunnel, with openings leading into the Dutch garden in the centre. The delicate pale green leaves contrast with the strong green of the 'battered' yew hedge growing below. The inset photograph shows a very decorative row of hornbeams grown as trees but shaped into cones, at the Military Museum, Bayeux, Normandy.

Hornbeam/Beech

Hornbeam is a reasonably fast grower which needs clipping annually. To the unknowing, it is easily mistaken for beech. Hornbeam is easy to grow in most soils and it is very successful as a hedge, although it can be topiarised into squarish shapes.

The same hedge as left, in winter, with its copper leaves glowing against the sky.

Pleached beech (looking very similar to hornbeam) grown as a stilt hedge against a mellow, old brick wall at Brickwall House, East Sussex.

Small holly-shaped leaves of berberis clipped into the shape of a pintail duck.

Lavender

Lavender responds well to a regular clipping regime if grown as a low hedge or a standard. Sadly, this means clipping before it actually flowers, but the results are well worthwhile. Sometimes it will be necessary to replace the plants after five years or so, if they become woody. Rosemary is an interesting alternative for low hedging or used as an accent at the end of a lavender hedge and is in fact commonly used as such in Mediterranean countries.

Holly

There are a huge number of holly varieties, with or without spiky leaves and in all shades of green and gold, or variegated as in the topiary shapes shown on this page.

Holly is very tough and not prone to disease. However, gloves have to be worn for clipping! It should not be allowed to grow too tall as clipping can then become very difficult for obvious reasons.

Berberis

This plant is more commonly used as boundary and burglar-proof hedging. It is fast-growing and quite easy to clip into shapes. The glossy green foliage resembles tiny, serrated holly leaves.

Pages 44–45 *An unusual design for a hedge. The copper beech has been cut into square uprights and interplanted with laurel. I was told that when the present owners moved in the tops of the copper beech had a busby shape (the previous owner had been a military man!), but this was eventually squared off to make for easier shaping.*

Variegated holly painstakingly clipped into a 'cakestand' shape, more commonly seen in yew.

A selection of mophead hollies. They look particularly attractive when covered in berries during winter.

Which child (or adult for that matter) could resist this charming 'tree' summer house complete with windows? Hornbeam has been trained over a simple frame to achieve a delightful garden building.

The simplicity of this pair of rectangles in clipped lavender, offset by a single tree in the centre of each, would be an easy idea to adapt or copy.

Instant Topiary Gardens

Topiary in pots is making a big comeback and it is not difficult to understand why – in a world where we all want to see instant results, this is a quick and easy way of creating a new look for your garden. It is also a perfect way of trying out new ideas as you can switch the topiary around until it looks just the way you want it. It is alright to change your mind! For small and bigger gardens alike, it is a perfect solution.

The plan opposite was created by Frances Traylen Martin for a small courtyard garden in the historical Kentish town of Tenterden. The owner already had two tables and garden benches and a large collection of herbs in clay pots. However, the garden needed 'pulling together' and Frances suggested adding some box bobbles in different sizes (see 1, 2, 3, 4, 5 and 6 on the plan), and accentuating the central axis (the path leading from the front door to the gate).

This relatively small adjustment is intended to lend the garden both a certain charm as well as structure. You will also see that on the left of the plan she has added a yew cone (7). The dramatic dark green stands out well against the brick wall and also leads the visitor's eye upwards.

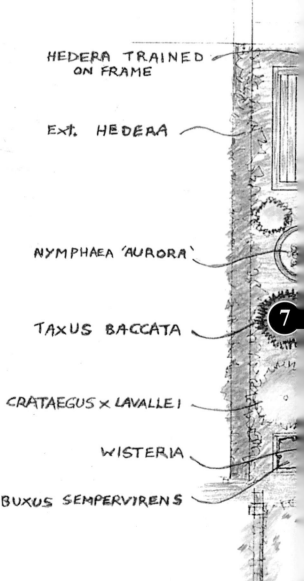

HEDERA TRAINED ON FRAME

Ext. HEDERA

NYMPHAEA 'AURORA'

TAXUS BACCATA

CRATAEGUS × LAVALLEI

WISTERIA

BUXUS SEMPERVIRENS

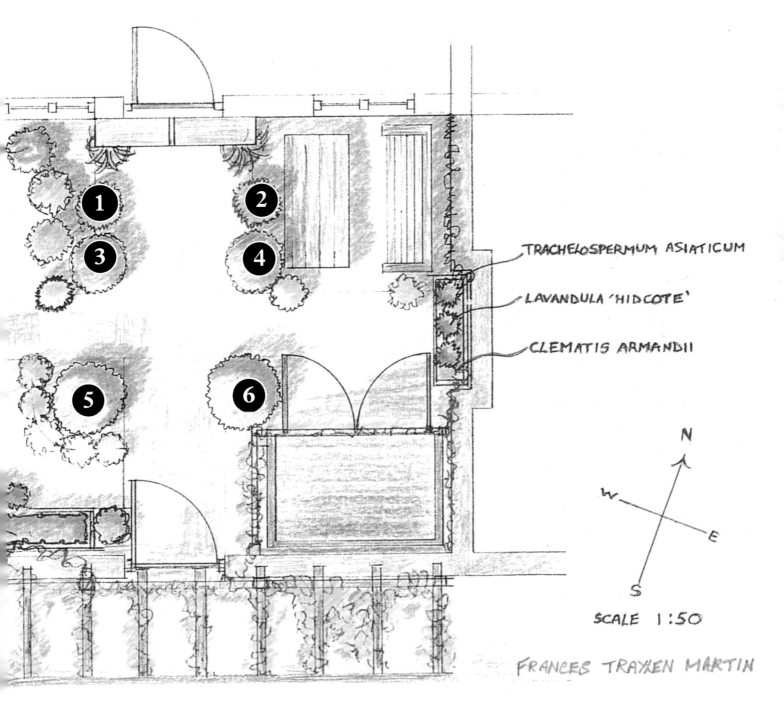

OWN-HOUSE TOPIARY GARDEN

TRACHELOSPERMUM ASIATICUM

LAVANDULA 'HIDCOTE'

CLEMATIS ARMANDII

SCALE 1:50

FRANCES TRAXEN MARTIN

49

On a visit to Belgium last year I got carried away and bought a large selection of box topiary in pots – bobbles of all sizes and four handsome cones. At the time I had no idea how they would all fit into my small garden, but felt that I could always pass any surplus on to friends.

However there was no need to worry: being on a number of different levels, the size of my garden was not a drawback, as I quickly realised that placing some of the pots on the steps leading from the terrace up to the lawn was a perfect way to display them. In fact, I now feel that I got great value out of my box investment and I enjoy being able to improve on my design and trying out new ideas picked up from other gardens I have visited.

This very small German garden reveals the owner's lifelong passion for box and, in addition, her sense of humour, wonderfully expressed through the way she places her plants. You can see how she has arranged the box bobbles in pots by size and created what I would describe as a stylized 'crocodile', which snakes its way over the terrace. Tomorrow she might decide to rearrange her box in a completely different way, according to mood!

Creating a Garden with Topiary

Topiary, in all its variety of shapes and forms, is used widely by garden designers, whether they are working on historical restoration projects, designing a completely new garden or potager, or bringing a rather neglected garden up-to-date and giving it a new lease of life.

Garden designer Frances Traylen Martin has for many years enjoyed creating bold topiary shapes in her own gardens, and now uses this experience when working on client briefs. A good example is the garden of the late fifteenth-century Anchor House in Lynsted village, on the chalky North Downs of Kent. This lovely oak-beamed house in the centre of the village is a Grade II listed building in a conservation area.

Up until 1997 the garden had no real plan and the semi-circular drive was taking up too much space. Lack of privacy was a problem, as the garden surrounded the house on two sides and was in full view from the road. Putting up a fence or a wall to screen the owners from curious passers-by was not an option, so the owners asked Frances for inspired alternatives.

Like many clients, they wanted a garden which would quickly look well-established. If possible, they also wanted to include plants of the same period as the house, including topiary and clipped hedges. Frances had to resolve a certain amount of conflicting needs: whilst wanting greater privacy in the garden, with places to sit, too much screening could pose a security risk.

Inspired by sixteenth-century gardens, Frances began by breaking the area up into a number of rough rectangular shapes. The terrace in front of the French window on the side was extended and enclosed by a low retaining wall. Steps were built leading up from the terrace to the parterre – the formal part of the layout.

View of Anchor House from the road, showing the lawn and newly-planted lavender hedge.

Opposite *Newly-planted hornbeam stilt hedge, just coming into leaf.*

The original design sketch for the topiary yew cones.

The same yew cones once planted, and a view of the new pergola with the stilt hedge beyond.

Frances achieved a feeling of privacy by enclosing the parterre with a stilt hedge of pleached hornbeams (which are easily grown in most soils) – these trees are specially grown and pruned so that the lower 1.5m (5ft) of trunk is kept bare as was popular in the sixteenth and seventeenth centuries. The remaining branches are trained on wires to grow out sideways and intertwine with those of the neighbouring trees. This is a style of hedge still often found in French parks and squares. Suitably trained trees are available from specialist nurseries, and it does not take long to achieve the desired effect once they are in their final growing position.

The great advantage of this growing method is that, although the trees create an enclosed space, there is the added pleasure of the view beyond, glimpsed between the tree trunks. You can see out, but it is difficult for people to see in.

Another version of a stilt hedge, this time combined with a dark green yew hedge below, can be seen in the Dutch garden at Ham House (see page 42). Here the concept has been taken one step further and the trees trained to grow into a marvellous green tunnel.

Back at Lynsted, four central beds were planted with box, *sempervirens* 'suffruticosa' and lavender *angustifolia* 'Hidcote'. Frances used quite small, bushy plants which, if well cared for and fed regularly, would grow into thick little hedges within two or three years. Each of the four beds was planted with a clipped standard bay laurel, *laurus nobilis* which functions as an accent and draws the eye to the overall scheme.

In front of the house, easily viewed from the sitting room, Frances works through her plans for a knot garden. The outlines of circles and squares are planted with dwarf box hedges. Topiarised box, yew and holly, set in gravel, provide both a centrepiece and interest at the entrances and corners.

A new gravel path edged with brick is created to link the garage and parking area with the front door. Here again, topiary comes into its own creating both focus and added interest: there are pyramid-shaped yews and osmanthus clipped into globes, while dwarf box hedging runs along each side of the path. The path from the small front gate is also flanked by trees, including two *Crataegus laevigata* which will eventually be clipped into lollipop or mophead shapes.

Newly-planted low box hedge. These small plants grow well once established and soon fill in to create the desired effect.

A Pair of Acorns

Alison had always wanted to try her hand at creating her own piece of topiary but was not sure where to start. So, as a first project, I suggested she should try out her creativity on a pair of box plants I had been keeping in pots for some years. I had never been able to decide how best to shape them and so had simply let them grow out into a pleasing, natural, fluffy-looking shape. Now it was time to do something more adventurous.

This is a fairly easy project for a beginner. It is also not too expensive to buy one or two box plants in pots and allow them to put on a little more growth for a season or two.

1 Alison takes quite some time to look at the plant from all sides. Topiary is a tactile activity, so she almost instinctively finds herself running her hands over each plant to get a 'feel' for it. This also releases the aromatic smell that the plant is famous for – undoubtedly one of the pleasures of clipping box. By touching it she gets a better idea of how much firm growth there is in the plant's heart, beyond the new shoots which give it its fullness.

In fact, it is very firm inside and so she decides to keep that inner shape as much as possible, only cutting back the new shoots. She feels there is enough growth to cut into a shape tapering downwards. With a 'skirt' left around the bottom edge you have what resembles an acorn, so it is an acorn shape that she decides to go for. Part of the skill of creating topiary is to learn to look at the natural inclination and growth of a plant and then judge to what shape it would best lend itself.

2 As the plants are fairly small, I recommend she uses a pair of large, sharp domestic scissors for cutting. These give her better control than secateurs or shears which are normally chosen for topiary. The size of the plant to be cut is the key factor in making your choice of cutting tool.

3 It is very important to be comfortable whilst clipping. Alison could have placed the pot of box on a small stand or an upturned crate, but she prefers to start by working at ground level. She sits on the ground with the pot between her legs so that she can get a good view of both sides of the plant. She wisely puts a sheet underneath to catch all the cuttings, to save time sweeping up once the job is finished.

4 Alison starts by cutting rather cautiously but soon gains more confidence and begins quite naturally to move around the plant. She turns her hand and the scissors round when necessary to get more purchase onto the area to be clipped.

5 To work towards the acorn shape, she needs to mark where to begin the wider shape, using a piece of string as a guide. Having completed the first box plant, she moves on to the second, placing it alongside the first so that she can match them up as closely as possible. She is now quite obviously feeling more confident and enjoying the sensation of creating a new shape out of a fragrant, bright green plant. This is fun!

6 Alison has another look at the two plants to make sure that she is getting the right finish, and that the two acorn shapes match. She gives just a few nips on the top and the sides to even them out and get a nice bit of rounding.

Here is the pair of finished acorns. Alison has created a basic shape which will grow and become fuller and firmer when it has had another cut or two. Cutting twice a year does not necessarily mean that the plant will stay the same size. If you are careful not to get carried away when trimming and just cut enough to build on the new shape and tidy it up, the acorns will actually grow larger – it is up to you to decide when to stop.

Potted box needs a change of earth, and possibly a larger pot, every three years. It should be fed frequently. Never allow it to dry out, and remember to water the top of the earth direct, as watering from the top of the plant means that water may not penetrate the leaves to reach the roots.

Clipping Bay Laurel Topiary

Bay laurel is the bay we also use for cooking and flavouring soups and stews. It is an evergreen and the oval, glossy dark green leaves are very attractive whether the plant is allowed to keep its natural shape or it is topiarised. In ideal conditions (full sun and well-drained soil) it can grow into an impressively tall tree. Although originally a Mediterranean plant, it will grow anywhere where the climate is mild. It is frost-hardy, although it is advisable to grow bay plants in pots which can be taken under cover during winter, if growing in an area prone to regular hard frosts.

In spring, the plant produces small fragrant white flowers, well before clipping becomes necessary around the end of May.

At first sight it does not look that easy to cut bay, but as the following pages show, it takes no more than a pair of ordinary, well-sharpened garden shears to do the job – and of course experience.

This self-sown bay laurel was cut into a fairly simple cube shape once it had reached a height of 0.6m (2ft) and was a good width. Four strong upward-growing stems – or leaders as they are called – were left unclipped so that they could grow out of the top of the cube. These eventually formed the multiple

Opposite The finished clipped bay topiary.

stem for the bobble on top of the base. All the side shoots on the leaders were cut off as they developed, leaving only the top growth which soon filled in and began to provide a rudimentary round shape. The following season this was clipped into a globe.

1 By May, this bay topiary is beginning to look distinctly shaggy. The crisp shape it kept all during the winter months needs restoring with a fairly hard cut. A cloth or sheet of plastic on the ground saves time when clearing up afterwards.

3 Clipping the lower section is easier and can be done from ground level whilst gradually working your way round the plant.

2 Keith starts at the top with the bobble. He uses a short ladder and, although bay can be quite tough to cut, he prefers a pair of ordinary sharp shears to an electric hedge-cutter. He is very experienced at clipping shapes and hedges, and you can clearly see how relaxed he is while cutting back to a clean, well-rounded shape. It is interesting to see that he does not hesitate to turn the shears round the 'wrong' way in order to get better purchase.

Standing on a ladder, however small, can be dangerous, so if the ground is at all uneven it is advisable to either have someone hold it steady for you or to use a ladder stabiliser.

4 The work does take a lot of concentration and it is easy to get totally absorbed and fail to notice that you are cutting too much off! It is a good idea to keep standing back from the plant to get an overall view and see how well you are achieving the desired outline.

Keith works systematically, clipping along the top of the lower shape before moving around the sides. Avoid stretching too far; you have to move your body along as you cut, keeping your eye on the amount you need to take off and ensuring that the final shape is level all round. Otherwise, you will end up with some unwanted dips. If you work at a steady speed you will avoid making errors you will later regret.

Working towards the lower half of the shape, Keith is pointing his shears downwards, still holding them in a relaxed way but very much in control. Then it is a question of carefully looking back over the whole area and tidying up the odd stem left sticking out to produce a crisp outline. This shape will now last through the winter until June, when the plant could have a light tidying clip before the main pruning towards the end of August.

Bizarre Topiary

There is no limit to the imagination in designing topiary and everyone's idea of the bizarre will be different. To my mind, some of the oddest shapes are those of everyday items. Strange effects may also result from the trimming of previously neglected, overgrown plants along the lines of their natural growth.

Some gardeners, inspired by Royal events such as jubilees and coronations, feel the urge to clip a lasting memory in the shape of a crown, as for instance in the picture below.

On the Kentish North Downs is a lovely old garden with this huge 3m (10 ft) yew hedge planted in the 1880s. The outsize crown on top was created to commemorate the Diamond Jubilee of Queen Victoria in 1898.

Opposite *This complex crown at Elvaston Castle, serves as an archway leading to another part of the garden, and creates a stunning contrast between the two varieties of yew. Amazingly, the golden yew was actually grafted onto the existing common variety by the very skilful hands of the head gardener in the nineteenth century.*

Hedges can be mysterious. Imagine walking through a door in an old garden wall and discovering some thirty or so huge yews clipped into cylinders, arranged in no apparent order, still wet with early dew and almost moving towards you in the morning mist. That was a mystical experience I had on a visit to Heslington Hall, York. There are also bizarrely shaped, ancient yews at Powys Castle which seem to race up the hillside, silhouetted against the darkened evening sky and full of secrets of their own. It is the combination of unusual shapes, vast scale and the extraordinary depth of colour, dark greens veering towards a dense blackness, which seems to give this wonderful plant a deep life and mystery all of its own.

Opposite *This yew hedge is an excellent example of how clipping can follow the lines of earlier neglect. It was not trimmed at all during the war, and subsequent cutting has tamed but not altered the natural growth lines. The resulting uneven, billowing effect is very dramatic.*

This pierced yew hedge full of strange curves and openings reminds children of a monster or even a dinosaur. I see it as a castle tower with the Loch Ness monster half in and half out! Was this design planned right at the start when planting, or did it evolve as the hedge grew, I wonder?

The original shape of yew or box will often inspire the creative gardener to clip in such a way that the shrub is teased into a familiar form – teapots, seats and chairs are quite common.

Garden seats are becoming quite a popular use of yew and other evergreens, and create a surprisingly tactile effect. The back of the seat above has two layers of different shades of green – yew and beech – which change in winter to green on brown. The plants curve around the back and sides of the seat and seem to welcome you into its embrace. The photograph below shows how this idea can be developed, in this case using variegated ivy which contrasts vividly with the multi-coloured brickwork behind.

A crown at Chirk Castle in Clwyd, Wales.
The bench inside this hollow crown gives some idea
of the extraordinary scale. I have never seen
anything like it elsewhere.

A beech table and yew chair at Chatsworth House in Derbyshire. This is a surprisingly homely idea for such a great estate, and may be intended for the children to play on.

This four-poster bed, also at Chatsworth, comprises ivy trained over a wooden frame. It even has a bedside table covered in ivy but this is not visible in the photograph.

This teapot shaped out of yew, is almost as high as the house. The dark green of the foliage against the yellow walls is most striking.

A pair of fairly ordinary tall thuya cylinders with a comical touch – some bright spark thought of placing a scarecrow on top.

A nursery field of spirals and jug-like shapes created from box plants. These are grown for the ready-made topiary market.

Perhaps the most bizarre of all – the almost ghostlike figure of a woman, in box grown through a frame.

Opposite *This photograph shows the knight of a newly-planted yew topiary chess set at Brickwall House, Northiam, East Sussex. It was planted over twenty years ago in this very old and historic garden, using golden yew for the white side and dark green yew for the black side. Special metal frames were designed and built for all the different figures, which were set in squares of coloured gravel. In the inset picture you can see very clearly how the yew plant is grown through the frame and then clipped to the outline, as in the main picture.*

74

Wondrous Creatures

English gardens seem to be part-icularly well suited to topiary birds and animals. Comical and endearing, they are hugely popular with children and adults alike! It is now possible to buy ready-made shapes for different birds and animals. With these the animal to be topiarised is allowed to grow through and is then cut back to give the desired shape.

Teddy bears are very popular in the Netherlands, where you see huge fields growing identical rows of these furry creatures. It can be quite a spooky experience.

Why not try creating your own favourite animal – the only limit is your imagination.

The exotic peacock, with or without a fantail in full glory, is perhaps the most commonly found topiarised bird. It perches on top of yew hedges, at gate entrances or on unusually elaborate multi-tier bases, as illustrated near right.

The bird on top of the massive hedge, illustrated opposite, is difficult to identify, but because of the scale of the topiary – the yew avenue must be well over 3m (10ft) tall – it looks quite incongruous sitting on top staring out over the valley.

The two inset photographs (2 and 3), show a rather smaller version of a peacock with fantail spread – this has been placed in a flowerbed, and looks very attractive. Chicken wire has been used to make the fan shape, through which the box is then grown.

I have not seen any topiary squirrels in an English garden, but they seem to be quite popular in Holland, where I photographed the two on this page. These charming creatures look wonderful on a lawn but it takes an artistic hand to make such a lifelike shape. Usually two or three plants are used and it takes a lot of careful tying of branches together to give the desired fullness.

A horse and rider can be created by growing a plant such as yew or privet through a frame. Interestingly, here there is a cone-shaped, topiarised variegated holly on the left and a colourful ivy trained over a column frame on the right. This portable topiary was exhibited at a horticultural event at the Château de Courson.

What about trying a snail when you are feeling more confident about your clipping skills? If you do not already have a well-grown yew or box plant whose shape would lend itself to such a project, try growing a number of plants fairly close to one another. Then encourage the shape you are aiming for by tying branches together and either leaving certain parts to grow out more when doing the annual big clip, or alternatively creating stepped sides to work towards the shape you want. The illustration above would be a good model to work from. This realistic topiary snail even has antennae.

This fiery dragon, complete with spray jets activated by anyone passing, has been created from some very old box bushes and some newly-planted box to create the curly tail.

Growing plants through frames is becoming more popular. The technique means that if you use ivy, for instance, you will soon have a realistic topiary animal such as this deer, seen at the annual plant fair at the Château de Courson, France. It was also in France that I saw a very convincing flock of topiary sheep, where again the plant used was ivy.

This wonderful topiary elephant keeps the peacock on page 77 company. It must have originally been clipped out of a field hedge, as it is made of a mixture of holly, yew and hawthorn. The combination gives the elephant a much-needed, subtle dimension, as apart from the ears it is clipped in relief, rather than being free-standing.

Because hawthorn is deciduous, he does tend to look a bit 'moth-eaten' in the winter, reviving again in the spring with the new growth

This row of huge teddybear-like figures in the gardens of Hall Place, Bexley, Kent, was planted in 1953 to commemorate the coronation of Queen Elizabeth. They were originally designed and clipped into heraldic figures, but over the decades they have lost their shape and now look quite extraordinary.

Making a Spiral

It took me some while to realise that topiary spirals are an optical illusion! It looks as if the plant is winding itself round and round to achieve that wonderful effect, but in fact the stem is straight and you are simply cutting the foliage into a spiral, as you can clearly see in the step-by-step photographs that follow.

Only the most intrepid topiarist would launch into making a spiral without a lot of previous thought and, above all, first watching someone experienced demonstrate the art at least once. These step-by-step photographs show a highly-experienced Dutch nurseryman using a short, very sharp knife to clip an upright-box plant into a spiral shape – it took him seven minutes flat! In my case I watched a spiral being clipped maybe twice or three times before I plucked up the courage to have a go myself.

Spirals are best displayed in pairs, placed perhaps on either side of a front door, preferably against a red brick or white wall where they can really stand out well and show off the finesse of their shape. If you are looking for a corkscrew spiral with multiple turns, for instance, then you will need to make far more cuts than for a gentle spiral.

Alternatively, you can plan a garden with a tall spiral as a focal point, either in the centre of the design or at the end of an avenue of hedging.

1 To make a spiral choose a well-grown plant with a straight stem, about 1m (3ft) tall. The most popular are box or yew, but others such as certain conifers would also be suitable.

2 Topiary is also about fitness and body flexibility and above all a good and well-practised eye. Bending well over the plant the topiarist firmly grasps it close to ground level and makes the first cut. He proceeds to clip away all the foliage at that spot. It is important to first work out exactly how low down this first cut should be, as the spacing of the rest of the cuts made at regular intervals up the stem, will be based on this first one.

3 Still leaning right over the plant, he works at shaping the foliage above the first cut, trimming away any superfluous leaves and branches to develop the spiral effect. He rounds off the curves where possible and all the while moves round the plant. He supports part of the plant between his knees to help him keep his balance.

4 Here you can see clearly how the spiral is taking shape. After this first clip it will look a little bare and need time to fill in. Meanwhile use your imagination as to the final result. Do not forget that you can decide on the type of spiral you prefer (loose and curvy as on page 87, or tight and corkscrew-like as demonstrated here) by varying the interval of clipped spaces.

5 Few of us will spend whole days doing one spiral after the other as this demonstrator sometimes does in the trimming season. Without regular experience, you will need to work far slower and also stand back to look at what we have done and make sure no ghastly mistakes have crept in!

6 Working his way up the plant, he repeats the cuts and the trims as often as is needed for the particular spiral effect he wants.

7 The spiral is nearly finished. Just a last little snip at the top and we can admire the snaking movement of the many turns winding up the stem of the box plant. It was all in a day's work for our demonstrator, but it takes rather more practice for ordinary mortals.

This elegant, gently curving box spiral in a container, has grown into its shape and no longer looks bare at the cut points. The tapering point at the top finishes it off to perfection.

Overleaf *An outsize golden yew topiary shape, left partly untrimmed, is reminiscent of vividly glowing tongues of flame. The contrast is all the more dramatic for being surrounded by solid-looking golden yew balls, all neatly clipped.*

This spiral can be seen at my local petrol station of all places! It is a tall box plant, around 2.5m (8ft) and quite unlike the other spirals mentioned in this chapter. The shape has been created by deep cuts at closely-spaced intervals. I suspect that the plant was originally grown as a cylinder and then only later transformed by an enthusiastic topiarist. It is said to have been planted in the 1950s and is growing out of paving stones.

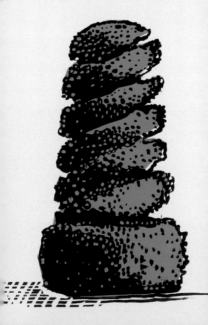

Acknowledgments

Photographic credits
L=left, R = Right, T=Top, B=Bottom,
I= Inset.

The author and publishers wish to thank everyone who kindly supplied either photographs, sketches, plans or line drawings for this book.

ILLUSTRATIONS
48/49: Plan by Frances Traylen Martin
54T: Design sketch by Frances Traylen Martin.
87I: Sketch by Chris Monk
90T/ 92T/ 94T: Sketches by Chris Monk after engravings

PHOTOGRAPHS
30I: Tom Wright, Doddington Place, Sittingbourne, Kent
42: Barbara Ingram-Monk, Bayeux, France
51: Mariele Suedholz, Westerstede Ocholt, Germany
54: Frances Traylen Martin

The following photographs are by the author:

1:     Elizabeth Braimbridge at Langley Boxwood Nursery, Liss, Hampshire
2:     Winchelsea, East Sussex
3:     Brickwall House, Northiam, East Sussex
4T: Langley Boxwood Nursery, Liss, Hampshire
4T: Elvaston Castle, Elvaston, Derbyshire
7:     Elvaston Castle, Elvaston, Derbyshire
8:     Clipsham Hall Avenue, Clipsham, Rutland
9:     Palace of Het Loo, Apeldoorn, Gelderland, Netherlands
10:    Fishbourne Roman Palace, Near Chichester, West Sussex
11:    Chiswick House, London
13:    Palace of Het Loo, Appeldoorn, Gelderland, Netherlands
13I: Private garden, Cowden, Kent
14:    Langley Box Nursery, Liss, Hampshire
14I: Van Klaveren Nursery, Boskoop, Netherlands
15:    Private garden, Belgium
16/17: Ashburnham House, Ashburnham, East Sussex
18:    Van Klaveren Nursery, Boskoop, Netherlands

19T: Elvaston Castle, Elvaston, Derbyshire
19B: Frans Hals Museum, Haarlem, Netherlands
21:    Goddards, Abinger Hammer, Surrey
22:    Huis Bingerden, Bingerden, Angerlo, Netherlands
23:    Peasmarsh Place, near Rye, East Sussex
25T: Huis Bingerden, Bingerden Angerlo, Netherlands
25:    Goddards, Abinger Hammer, Surrey
26:    Hall Place, Bexley, Kent
27:    Ashburnham House, Ashburnham, East Sussex
28:    Piet Oudolf Nursery, Netherlands
30/31: Private garden, Kent
32:    Middachten, De Steeg, Gelderland, Netherlands
33:    Elvaston Castle, Elvaston, Derbyshire
34:    Palace of Het Loo, Apeldoorn, Gelderland, Netherlands
35:    Hall Place, Bexley, Kent
36:    Winchelsea, East Sussex
37:    Private garden, Zeeland, Netherlands
38T: Private garden, Kent
38B: Private garden, Southborough, Kent
39T: Private garden, Winchelsea, East Sussex
39B: Private garden, Winchelsea, East Sussex
40BL: Huis Bingerden, Bingerden, Angerlo, Netherlands
40T/B: Private garden, Winchelsea, East Sussex
41:    Cabbages & Kings, Hadlow Down, East Sussex
42:    Ham House, Richmond, Surrey
42TI: Military Museum, Bayeux, France
43L: Brickwall House, Northiam, East Sussex
43TR: Brickwall House, Northiam, East Sussex
43BR: Private Garden, near Rye, East Sussex
44/45: Private garden, Crowborough, East Sussex
46TB: Highfield Hollies Nursery, Liss, Hampshire
47:    Huis Bingerden, Bingerden, Angerlo, Netherlands
47B: Private garden, Zeeland

50:    Private garden, Winchelsea, East Sussex
51:    Private garden, Westerstede Ocholt, Germany
52-53: Anchor House, Lynsted, Kent
56-61: Alison Couch in her Crowborough garden, East Sussex
62-65: Keith Bignall in a Winchelsea garden, East Sussex
66:    Private garden, Kent
67:    Elvaston Castle, Elvaston, Derbyshire
68:    Doddington Place, nr. Sittingbourne, Kent
69:    Private garden, Kent
70TL: Chirk Castle, Clywd, Wales
70TR: Chatsworth House, Buxton, Derbyshire
70B: Elvaston Castle, Elvaston, Derbyshire
71TB: Chatsworth House, Buxton, Derbyshire
72:    Cottage garden, Chiddingstone Hoath, Kent
73:    Van Klaveren Nursery, Boskoop, Netherlands
74:    Private garden, Veer, Netherlands
75:    Brickwall House, Northiam, East Sussex
76/77: All private gardens, Kent
78T: Huis Bingerden, Bingerden, Angerlo, Netherlands
78I: Van Klaveren Nursery, Boskoop, Netherlands
79:    Garden Fair, Château de Courson, France
80T: Huis Bingerden, Bingerden, Angerlo, Netherlands
80B: Houghton House, Stockbridge, Hampshire
81:    Garden Fair, Château de Courson, France
81:    Private garden, Ide Hill, Kent
82/83: Hall Place, Bexley, Kent
84/86: Van Klaveren Nursery, Boskoop, Netherlands
87:    Langley Boxwood Nursery, Liss, Hampshire
88/89: Elvaston Castle, Elvaston, Derbyshire

Opposite *Drawing made from an old photo of 'Fortifications' clipped in yew in the gardens of Old Place, Lindfield, Sussex. The gardens were designed in the late nineteenth century.*

The author owes a great debt of gratitude to the many friends and garden-owners who have shown her their lovely gardens and permitted her to photograph them. In particular she wishes to mention Baroness Digna Sweerts de Landas, with whom she has spent countless happy hours planning their numerous garden trips – including a unique tour of the gardens of Moscow – and has been privileged to discover the charming hidden gardens, often by bike, in the Dutch countryside. Digna's husband, Jaap, also deserves my heartfelt thanks, for always being so supportive and understanding of our unbounded enthusiasm and ambitious travel plans! Thank you also for your permission to photograph the charming pair of birds shown on page 37.

Many people have influenced the making of this book, both directly and indirectly – sometimes without even being aware of it. But a special mention should also be made of Elizabeth and Mark Braimbridge and Countess Véronique Goblet d'Alviella, the founders of the European Box and Topiary Society (EBTS), which helped me to really focus on topiary and discover how much it means to me. It is a splendid organisation of which I am proud to be a founder member and which has imperceptibly become a real part of my life and work.

This book would also not have been possible without the generous help of box expert Elizabeth Braimbridge, who supplied invaluable advice and information for the chapter on box; Frances Traylen Martin who so generously allowed me to use her garden design material for Anchor House, Mr and Mrs R. Sabin, who gave their kind permission to reproduce the plans and photos; and of course Alison, Keith and Mr van Klaveren who allowed me to photograph them stage by stage, whilst clipping topiary plants. I am very grateful to all of you for your kindness and willingness to help me put this book together.

My publishers, Search Press, and all my long-standing friends who have helped me to make this book a reality deserve particular mention – Roz Dace and Chantal Porter, my Editors, as well as Martin de la Bédoyère, Publisher, have seen me through the inevitable difficult moments and always won over with humour and total professionalism.

Finally, I wish to express my thanks and appreciation to both Cindy Stevens, who helped me with editing, checking proofs and indexing, and graphic designer, Chris Monk, of Yellowduck Design & Illustration, who has always been totally unflappable and has designed the book to look in a way that I would never have believed possible

when starting out on this project.

Without all the wonderful gardens, there would of course never have been a book, so I would like to thank most warmly the following people and organisations for permitting me to reproduce the photographs of their gardens and for all their kind encouragement: Mr John Morgan, Mrs Mary Frewen Parsons and the Governors of Frewen College, Derbyshire County Council, the Forestry Commission, the Curator of the Royal Palace of Het Loo, English Heritage, Mrs Ghan Bloemers, Mr van Klaveren, the Ashburnham Christian Trust, Mme S. Meyer-de-Feyter, the Curator of the Frans Hals Museum, Haarlem, The Landmark Trust, Viscount Davenport, Bexley Council, Mr Piet Oudolf, Mrs Amicia Oldfield, The Curator Stichting Kasteel Middachten, Mrs A. Dekker, David Joyce, Christopher Lloyd, Mariele Suedholz, Mr Peter Janes, Mrs D. Crispin Shemeld, Mrs Aggy Boshof, Mrs Ryl Nowell, The National Trust, Mrs Sandra Pawsey, Mr and Mrs Roger Knight, Mrs Louise Bendall, His Grace the Duke of Devonshire, Mrs A. Busk, Mr John Lode and Mr Edward Lode, Mr V. Fleming, 5Mr. & Mrs C. Ross, Roger Binning, Mme van Weede, the Sussex Archeological Society, Phillip Goodwin and Lady FitzWalter.

Gardens to Visit

An eighteenth-century design for avenues on a massive scale.

This list of gardens is by no means exhaustive. Many are owned by the National Trust, some are owned privately but open on certain days during the year either under the National Gardens Scheme (NGS) or on a local Open Gardens Day, others are open to groups only by prior appointment. Details of the NGS scheme can be found in the yellow NGS guides, available from local libraries, newsagents and bookshops. *Hudson's Historic Houses and Gardens* is an excellent companion reference work for further details of the gardens in the UK listed here, as well as for other places of interest to the topiary enthusiast. If you do not have these guides to hand, it is advisable always to ring and check the opening times before setting out.

ENGLAND

Berkshire
Dorney Court, Dorney, nr Windsor
  01628 604638

Buckinghamshire
Ascott, Wing, nr Leighton Buzzard
  (Bedfordshire) 01296 688242
Chenies Manor, Chenies, nr Chesham
  01494 762888
Cliveden, Taplow, nr Maidenhead
  01628 605069

Cheshire
Arley Hall, Arley, nr Northwich
  01565 777353
Little Moreton Hall, Congleton
  01260 272018
Peover Hall, Over Peover, nr Knutsford
  01565 632358
Tatton Park, Knutsford
01565 654822

Cumbria
Levens Hall, nr Kendal 01539 560321

Derbyshire
Chatsworth, Buxton 01246 582204
Elvaston Castle, Elvaston, nr Derby
  01332 571342
Hardwick Hall, Doe Lea,
  nr Chesterfield 01246 850430
Melbourne Hall, Melbourne
  01332 862502
Renishaw Hall, nr Chesterfield
  01777 860755

Dorset
Athelhampton House, nr Dorchester
  01305 848363
Cranborne Manor, Cranborne,
  nr Wimborne 01725 517248
Parnham House, nr Beaminster
01308 862204

Essex
Saling Hall, Saling, nr Great Braintree
  01371 850243

Gloucestershire
Barnsley House, Barnsley,
nr Cirencester 01285 740281
Hidcote Manor, nr Chipping Camden
  01386 438333
Painswick Churchyard, Painswick,
nr Stroud
Rodmarten Manor, nr Cirencester
  01285 841253
Sudeley Castle, Winchcombe,
  nr Cheltenham 01242 603197
Westbury Court Garden, Westbury-
  upon-Severn, nr Gloucester
  01452 760461

Hampshire
Highfield Hollies, Liss, nr Petersfield
  01730 892372
Houghton Lodge, nr Stockbridge
  01264 810177
Langley Boxwood Nursery, Rake, Liss,
  nr Petersfield 01730 894467
Mottisfont Abbey, Mottisfont,
  nr Romsey 01794 340757
Tudor House Museum, Bugle Street,
  Southampton 01703 635904

Hereford & Worcester
Hanbury Hall, nr Droitwich
  01527 8221214

Hertfordshire
Hatfield House, Hatfield 01707 262823

Kent

Brenchley Church, Brenchley,
nr Paddock Wood
Doddington Place, Doddington,
nr Sittingbourne 01795 886101
Goodnestone Park, Goodnestone
01304 840107
Groombridge Place, Groombridge,
nr Tunbridge Wells 01892 863999
Hall Place, Bexley 01322 526574
Hever Castle, Hever, nr Edenbridge
01732 865224
Penshurst Place, Penshurst,
nr Tonbridge 01892 870307
Sissinghurst Castle, Sissinghurst,
nr Cranbrook 01580 715330
Squerryes Court, Westerham
01959 562345
Yaldham Manor, Sevenoaks
01732 762888

London

Chiswick House, Burlington Lane, W4
0181 955 0508
Museum of Garden History, Lambeth
Palace Road, SE1 0171 261 1891

Norfolk

Blickling Hall, Blickling, nr Aylsham
01263 733084
Felbrigg Hall, Felbrigg, nr Cromer
01263 837444

Northamptonshire

Coton Manor, Guilsborough,
nr Northampton 01604 740219
Holdenby House, Holdenby,
nr Northampton 01604 770074

Northumberland

Herterton House, nr Cambo (Morpeth)
01670 774278
Seaton Delaval Hall, Seaton Sluice,
nr Whitley Bay 0191 237 3040

Oxfordshire

Beckley Park, Beckley, nr Oxford
Blenheim Palace, Woodstock
01993 811091

Rutland

Clipsham Hall, Clipsham

Somerset

Claverton Manor (The American
Museum), Bath 01225 460503
Tintinhull Garden, Tintinhull, Yeovil
01935 822545

Staffordshire

Biddulph Grange Garden, Biddulph,
nr Stoke-on-Trent 01782 517999

Suffolk

Helmingham Hall, Helmingham,
Ipswich 01473 890363

Surrey

Goddards, Abinger Common, Dorking
01306 730871
Ham House, Ham, nr Richmond
0181 940 1950
Hampton Court Palace, Hampton
Wick 0181 781 9500

Sussex East

Brickwall House, Northiam, nr Rye
01797 223329
Cabbages & Kings, Hadlow Down
01825 830552
Great Dixter, Northiam, nr Rye 01797
252878

Sussex West

Fishbourne Roman Palace,
nr Chichester 01243 785859
Nymans Gardens, Handcross,
nr Haywards Heath 01444 400321
West Dean Gardens, West Dean,
Chichester 01243 811301

Wiltshire

Bowood House, nr Calne
01249 812102
Heale Garden, Woodford, nr Salisbury
01722 782504
Heywood House Lodge, Heywood,
nr Trowbridge
Longleat House, nr Warminster
01985 844400

Yorkshire

Harewood House, Harewood, Leeds
0113 288 6331

SCOTLAND

Grampian

Crathes Castle, Banchory (Aberdeen)
01330 844525
Hazelhead Park, nr Aberdeen
Pitmedden Garden, Ellon, nr Aberdeen
01651 842352

Perthshire

Drummond Castle, Crieff 01764 681257

Roxburghshire

Floors Castle, Kelso 01573 223333

WALES

Clwyd

Chirk Castle, Chirk, nr Wrexham
01691 777701
Erddig, nr Wrexham 01978 355314

Gwynedd

Plas-in-Rhiw, Rhiw, nr Pwllheli

Powys

Powis Castle, nr Welshpool
01938 554338

EIRE

County Down

Mount Stewart, nr Newtonnards

County Offaly

Birr Castle, Birr

County Wicklow

Powerscourt Estate, Enniskerry

AUSTRIA

Belvedere Palace, Vienna
Schoenbrunn Palace, Vienna

BELGIUM

Château de Belúil, Belúil, Hainaut
Parc des Topiares, Durbuy,
Prov de Liége

FRANCE

Château de Chenonceaux,
Indre-et-Loire
Château de Courances, Essonne
Château de Hautfort, Périgord
Château de Versailles, Yvelines
Château de Villandry, Indre-et-Loire
Eyrignac, Salignac, Dordogne
Vaux-le-Vicomte, Seine-et-Marne

GERMANY

Herrenhausen, Hanover, Lower Saxony
Schwerzingen, Baden-Württemburg
Veitshoechheim, Bavaria

ITALY

Castello Baldaino, Montalto, Lombardy
Giardiano dei Giusti, Verona, Veneto
Villa Allegri Arvedi, Cuzzoni, Veneto
Villa Gamberaia, Settignano, Tuscany
Villa Garzoni, Collodi, Tuscany
Villa Lante, Bagnaia, Lazio

NETHERLANDS

Frans Hals Museum, Haarlem
Huis Bingerden, Ligging, Angerlo
Kastel Amerongen, Amerongen,
Utrecht
Kasteel Twickel, Delden, Almelo
Kasteel de Vanenburg, Putten,
Gelderland
Middachten, De Steeg, Gelderland
Raadhuis Sparrendael, Driebergen,
Utrecht
Rijksmuseum Paleis Het Loo,
Apeldoorn, Gelderland
De Wiersse, Vorden, Gelderland

PORTUGAL

Quinta da BaÁalhoa, Estremadura
Palace of Fronteira, Lisbon
Vila Marcus, Tras-os-Montes
Bishop's Palace, Castelo Branco

Index

A drawing based on an eighteenth-century engraving of the gardens of Kuskovo Palace, Moscow. Although the amusing niches filled with topiary figures in the foreground no longer exist, the original layout of the gardens is still in place today and visitors can see an elaborate design of beech hedges running down on either side of the gardens.

Page references in bold indicate main references.

acorns (topiary) 56–61
Alexander, Amos 8
American colonists 12
Anchor House (Lynsted, Kent) 52–5
animals (topiary) 8, 11, 76, **78–83**
see also individual animal entries
arches, archways see architectural shapes
architectural shapes 11, 23–4, 26, 32
archways 11, 24, 66, 96
buttresses 23–4, 26
castellations 24, 39
crenellations 24
domes 40
fortifications 91
piers 23
Austria 93

Bagnaia (Italy) 11
balls (topiary) 12, 86
Baroque period 8, 12
'battering' 24, 42
bay laurel see laurel
Bayeux (Normandy, France), Military Museum 42
beech 43, 70–1, 94
Belgium 24, 50, 93
berberis 43, 46
birds (topiary) 36–7, 76–7

Blenheim 15
bobbles (topiary) 29, 48, 50–1, 62, 64
bonemeal 32
Boskoop (Netherlands) 11
box 4, 8, **12–19**, 48, 50–1, 55–61, 70, 73–4, 80, 84, 86–7
Buxus sempervirens 12
'suffruticosa' 55
clipping 16, 55–60, 84–6
edging with 12
feeding 15, 32, 60
frost, protection from 16, 40
golden 19
growing conditions for 15, 60
mulching 32
'plucking' 16
pots, growing in 15, 56–61
re-potting 15, 60
transplanting 32
variegated 19
varieties of 12
watering 15
Brickwall House (Northiam, E. Sussex) 43, 74–5
broderies 11–12
Brown, 'Capability' 15
buttresses see architectural shapes
Buxus sempervirens see box

cakestands (topiary) 23, 46
castellations see architectural shapes
Chatsworth House (Derbyshire) 71
chess sets (topiary) 74–5
chicken wire, use of 15, 76
China 15
Chirk Castle (Clwyd) 70
Chiswick House, West London 11
clipping see box, laurel, bay
Clipsham Hall (Rutland) 8
coloured earth 12
cones (topiary) 8, 12, 23–4, 32, 42, 48, 50, 54, 79
containers 40 see also pots
copper beech 44–6
Courson, Château de (France) 79, 81
Crataegus laevigata see hawthorn
crenellations see architectural shapes
crowns (topiary) 32, 66–7, 70
'curls' (topiary) 19
cut work see parterres
cutting 6, 60 see also box, clipping, laurel, bay, yew
cylinders (topiary) 40, 69, 71, 75
cypress 8

Dark Ages 10
deer (topiary) 81
designing 6, 24, 46, 50
domes see architectural shapes
Dragon 80
duck, pintail (topiary) 43
Dutch see Netherlands

eighteenth century 11, 12, 15, 92, 96
Eire 93
elephant (topiary) 81
Elvaston Castle (Derbyshire) 7, 33, 66–7
England 11–12, 15, 76, 92–3
English see England
engravings 11, 96
Europe 6, 11

feeding 15, 32, 60
fertilizer, burning effect 15
fifteenth century 11, 52
Fishbourne Palace (West Sussex) 8, 10
formal gardens 10–12, 15
fortifications see architectural shapes
four-poster bed (topiary) 71
foxes (topiary) 32
frames 71, 74, 79, 81
France 11–12, 15, 23, 25, 55, 81, 93
Frans Hals Museum (Haarlem, Netherlands) 19

French see France
frost 16, 20, 40, 62
garden seats 23, 70
geometric shapes 10, 12, 17, 34–5, 40
Germany 15, 93
globes (topiary) 11, 24, 40–1, 55
Goddards (Surrey) 20–21
Goodnestone Park (Kent) 96
gravel 12, 19, 55
  coloured 74

Hall Place (Bexley, Kent) 82
Ham House (Richmond, Surrey) 11, 41, 55
  Dutch garden 42
hawthorn 6, 36–7, 78, 81
  Crataegus laevigata 36, 55
hedgecutters, electric 6, 16, 39, 64
hedging
  berberis 46
  box 55
  copper beech 44–6
  hawthorn 6
  hornbeam 42–3, 53, 55
  laurel 44–6
  lavender 52
  low 10, 12, 46, 55
  pierced 69
  screen 11
  stilt 42–3, 52–5
  yew 6, 20, 23–4, 26, 28–9, 32, 66, 74–7
herbs 10, 12
Heslington Hall (York) 69
Het Loo (Apeldoorn, Netherlands) 8–9, 11–13
holly 46, 55, 78, 81
  clipping 46
  variegated 46, 79
holm oak 36
honeysuckle 36
hornbeam 42–3, 52–3, 55
  clipping 43
  growing conditions for 43
  pleached 55
horse and rider (topiary) 79
hounds (topiary) 32
hunting scenes (topiary) 8

Ide Hill (Kent) 81

initials (topiary) 8
instant results 49
Italy 10, 12, 93
ivy
  trained (using a frame) 70, 81
  variegated 71

Jefferson, Thomas 12
Jekyll, Gertrude 20

Joyce, David 29
Kensington Palace, Orangery Gardens 40
keyholes (topiary) 25
kitchen gardens 12
knife, for clipping 84
knot gardens 10, 12, 55
Kuskovo Palace (Moscow) 94

ladders 64
  stabilisers for 64
laurel 44–5
  bay 40, 46, 55, 62–5
    clipping 62–5
    frost, protecting from 40, 62
    growing conditions for 40, 62
    Laurus nobilis 55
    pruning 65
  Portuguese 40–1
Laurus nobilis see laurel, bay
lavender 46–7, 52
  angustifolia 'Hidcote' 55
  clipping 46
Le Nôtre 11
leaders 29, 38, 62
light, effect of 24–5
Lloyd, Nathaniel 23
lollipops (topiary) see mopheads
London 6, 11, 40, 93
Lutyens, Sir Edwin 20

manure, farmyard 32
Marot, Daniel 6
maze 24, 29
medieval period 10, 12
Moore, Henry 38
mopheads (topiary) 36, 40, 46, 55
mushrooms (topiary) 38
myrtle 8, 10–11

nasturtiums 34
Netherlands, The 11–12, 19, 36, 55, 76, 78, 93
niches 23–4, 94
nineteenth century 7, 66, 91
nurseries 11, 55

obelisks (topiary) 11, 34
Old Place (Lindfield, W. Sussex) 94
osmanthus 55

parterres 11–12, 15, 19, 52
  à l'anglaise 12
  of cut work 12
  de broderie 12
patterns 10–12, 17
peacocks (topiary) 32, 76
photography 6
piers (topiary) see architectural shapes
Pilgrims Way (Kent)
Pitmedden (Aberdeenshire) 15
planting plans 7, 10, 48
pleaching 55
Pliny the Elder 8
portable topiary see ready-made topiary
Portugal 15, 93
Portuguese laurel see laurel
Powis Castle (Powys) 69
pots 15, 48, 51, 62
  see also box, pots
privet 38–9, 79
  common dark green 39
  golden 39
  maintenance of 39
  pruning 24, 26, 28, 65
pyramids (topiary) 11, 55

ready-made topiary 73, 79
relief work 81
Renaissance, Italian 10
Romans 8, 10
rootballs 15
rosemary 10, 46

saucers, terracotta 15
scarecrow (topiary) 71
scissors 57–8
Scotland 93
scorching 16, 40
screens see hedging
Seaton Delaval Hall (Northumberland) 15
secateurs 57
Second World War 29, 75
seventeenth century 8, 11–12, 15, 55
shadows, effect of 24–5
shapes, creating 56–9, 68, 80, 84–6
shears, garden 6, 16, 57–8, 62–65
sheep (topiary) 81
ships (topiary) 8, 11
sixteenth century 12, 52, 55
snail (topiary) 80
Spain 15
spirals (topiary) 12, 73, 84–87
squirrels (topiary) 78
statuary 23–4

stilt hedges see hedging
string, as guide for cutting 16, 59
Strong, Dr Roy 23
sundials (topiary) 12
Sweden 15

table and chair (topiary) 71
Taxus aurea see yew, golden
Taxus baccata see yew, common
teapots (topiary) 68, 70, 72–3
teddy bears (topiary) 76, 82–3
Tenterden (Kent) 48
theatres, open-air 24, 29
thuya 73
tools 16, 57, 63–4, 84
Traylen Martin, Frances 48, 52, 55
Tuckahoe (USA) 12
tunnels (topiary) 11, 42, 55
tying (branches) 78, 80

Villa Lanta, Bagnaia (Italy) 11

Wales 93
windows (topiary) 24
wire, use of 15, 55
Wise, Henry 15

yew 4, 6–8, 11, 20–35, 46, 48, 54–5, 66–76, 78, 80–81, 84, 86, 91
  common (*Taxus baccata*) 20, 23, 66–7
  cutting 24, 26, 29, 75
  English see yew, common
  fastigiate see yew, Irish
  feeding 32
  fertilising 28
  frost, protecting from 20
  golden (*Taxus aurea*) 7, 24, 26, 33, 66–7, 74–5, 78, 86
  growing conditions for 23
  growth rate 23
  hedges see hedging
  heeling-in 20
  Irish 26
  maintenance of 20
  mulching 28, 32
  pruning 24, 26, 29
  renovation 26, 29
  varieties of 23
  wind-barrier, as a 20, 24

Bibliography

A new knot garden, at Goodnestone Park in Kent, created in 1999 especially to celebrate the Millennium. The designer, Charlotte Molesworth, has followed a tradition dating back to Roman times as described by Pliny, where letters and figures are created out of topiary plants.

Braimbridge, E and Meyer, B, *Box*, Sage Press, 1998

Carr, David, *Topiary & Plant Sculpture*, Crowood, 1989

E.Clarke & G Wright, *English Topiary Gardens*, Phoenix Illustrated (Weidenfeld & Nicholson), 1988

Clevely, AM, *Topiary: The Art of Clipping Trees & Ornamental Hedges*, Collins, 1988

Curtis, Charles H & Gibson, W, *The Book of Topiary*, Lane, 1904

Gallup, Barbara, *The Complete Book of Topiary*, Arlington, 1989

Hadfield, Miles, *Topiary & Ornamental Hedges*, A. & C. Black, 1971

Hendy, Jenny, *Quick and Easy Topiary*, Little Brown, 1996

Jennings, Anne and Whalley, Robin, *Knot Gardens & Parterres*, Barn Elms, 1998

Joyce, David, *Topiary and the Art of Training Plants*, Frances Lincoln, 1999

Lacey, Geraldine, *Creating Topiary*, Garden Art Press, 1987

Meyer, B, and Stevens, C, *Yew*, Sage Press, 1999

Riley Hammer, Patricia, *The New Topiary – Imaginative Techniques from Longwood Gardens*, Garden Art Press, 1991.

Stewart, Cecil, *Topiary: An Historical Diversion*, Golden Cockerel Press, 1954.

Topiarius Magazine, available from the European Box and Topiary Society (EBTS) c/o Sage Press, P.O.Box No. 1, Rye, East Sussex TN36 4ZX

Additional information

Some useful addresses for topiary enthusiasts:

Crown Topiary, 234 North Road, Hertford, SG14 2PW

European Box and Topiary Society (EBTS), Membership Secretary, P.O.Box 21897, London SW6 2FY

Highfield Hollies, Highfield Farm, Hatch Lane, Liss, Hampshire, GU33 7NH

National Collection – Buxus, Langley Boxwood Nursery, Rake, Liss, Hampshire GU33 7JL

River Garden Nurseries, Troutbeck, Otford, Sevenoaks, Kent TN14 5PH